Russell Stannard

The Lab Cats Get up Steam

A look at what things are made of

Illustrated by
Bill Ledger

MARSHALL PUBLISHING • LONDON

Dear Parent

This **Lab Cats** book introduces the idea of materials and their properties to young children in an enjoyable way as they follow the adventures of a gang of cats. It can be read aloud while a younger child follows the words and pictures, or an older child can read it alone. Each experiment that the cats do is followed by the correct answers. Ask your child to give the answer before turning the page to see what the Lab Cats did. Any new or difficult scientific words are explained in "What the Words Mean" on page 36. Happy reading!

A Marshall Edition
Created, edited and designed by
Marshall Editions Ltd
The Orangery
161 New Bond Street
London W1S 2UF
www.marshallpublishing.com

First published in the UK in 2001 by
Marshall Publishing Ltd

10 9 8 7 6 5 4 3 2 1

ISBN 1 84028 419 6

Originated in the UK by Hilo
Printed in Portugal by Printer Portuguesa

Editor Rosalind Beckman
Managing Designer: Caroline Sangster
Art Director: Simon Webb
Editorial Manager: Kate Phelps
US Consultant: Dr Roberta Butler
Production: Victoria Grimsell &
Christina Schuster

At night, the caretaker's cat wandered the school corridors. She could hear the young cats outside fighting and knocking over dustbin lids.

"It ought not be allowed," she grumbled, "roaming the streets after dark and getting into mischief."

One evening, the din from the street was so loud that the caretaker's cat could stand it no longer.

"I'll put a stop to it myself," she muttered. She went out, stood on the steps and called at the top of her voice.

"All you cats, over here! At once! It's school time!"

She sounded just like one of the teachers.

One by one, the cats crept out from the shadows, curious to learn what the noise was about.

"Follow me," she said. She led them through the cat flap in the door and into the science laboratory.

"In future there will be no more hanging around street corners. You will be here, doing something useful: Science."

"Science!?" the cats exclaimed.

"That's right. Names, please…"

The cats did as they were told and called out their names, one at a time.

Science is learning about the world by studying, looking and trying things out.

"You at the end, Swot. No need to start writing yet. Wait till the lesson begins."

"All right, Miss… er, Miss…," said Swot.

"Yeah," Ginger broke in. "What do we call you? The Professor? Or maybe Prof, for short?"

The caretaker's cat smiled. "Prof will be fine."

"This morning, the school children were learning about different materials. 'Materials' include things such as wood, metal and plastic. Some are found in nature; others have to be made," explained the Prof.

"Here are some objects and nine labels. Each label has the name of a different material. I want you to decide which label goes with which object or objects."

The place was quickly in uproar.

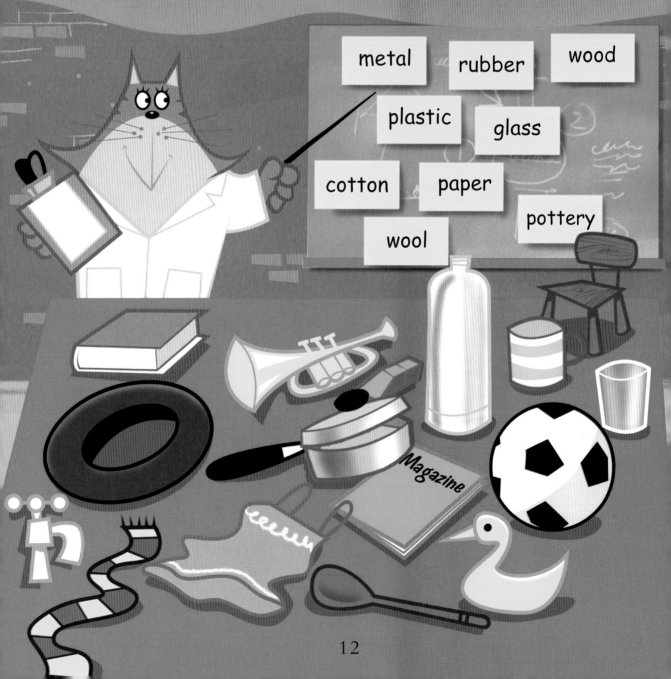

metal   rubber   wood

plastic   glass

cotton   paper

pottery

wool

See if you can match the labels to the objects.

My favourite colour!

13

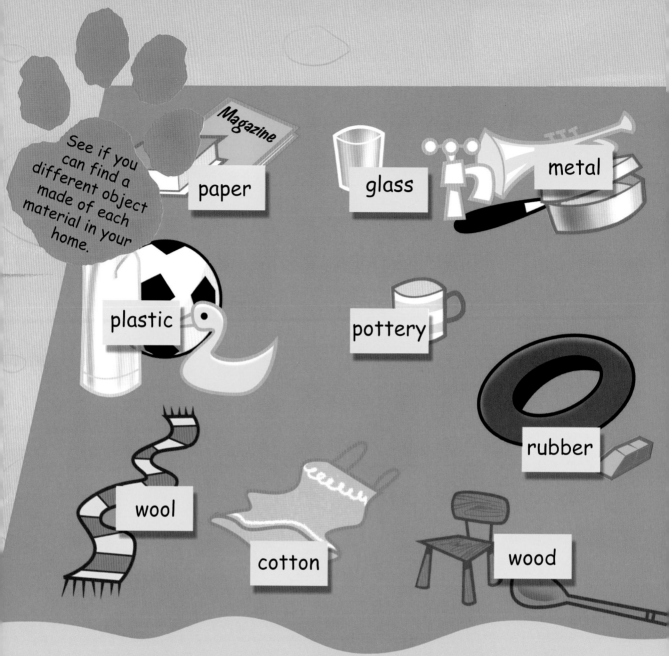

See if you can find a different object made of each material in your home.

Magazine

paper

glass

metal

plastic

pottery

rubber

wool

cotton

wood

After a lot of arguing, the cats finished their project. They all looked very pleased with themselves.

"That was brilliant," said Ginger.

"Yeah, I reckon we did all right there," said Basher. "We make a good gang."

"Prof," said Lucky, "can we give our gang a name? How about… the Laboratory Cats?"

"Too long," Basher butted in. "Let's be the Lab Cats!"

"I know, I know!" cried Swot excitedly.

And before anyone else could say a word, he had filled in all the spaces.

"That's not fair," said Fluff, "I didn't have time."

"Anyway," said Basher, "Know-it-all has got it wrong. Drainpipes are made of iron."

"That's also right," said the Prof, "Swot has given us just one answer."

That would have been a good answer, too.

"Now take a look at these objects," continued the Prof. "Who is able to tell me *why* they are made of different materials? Let's finish off the sentences on the board. We need to choose the right reason – I have already done one for you."

Can you finish off the other sentences?

Swot! Give the others a chance this time.

Bubble wrap is used for packaging because...

it is soft.

Steel is used for keys because...

Glass is used for windows because...

Rubber is used for elastic bands because...

Wool is used for clothing because...

Watch what you're doing, Ginger!

Bubble wrap is used for packaging because...
  it is soft.

Steel is used for keys because...
  it is hard.

Glass is used for windows because...
  you can see through it.

Rubber is used for elastic bands because...
  it is stretchy.

Wool is used for clothing because...
  it keeps the warmth in.

And fish is used in cat food because... it tastes good!

Can you guess why footballs aren't made of glass?

"Perfect!" declared the Prof. "Well done!"

"Purr…fect, did you say?" asked Lucky, and started purring happily. The others joined in.

"Yes, yes," said the Prof. "That's enough of that. You did really well, but there is a lot more I want to show you."

PURRRR

PURRRR

I'm hungry. Anyone seen a mouse?

"Materials can be either solids, liquids or gases. *Solids* stay the same shape and size. *Liquids* stay the same size, but can flow and change their shape to fit whatever they are placed in. *Gases* can change both their shape and size to fit any space."

"Here are six things: oil, milk, a hammer, a chair, air and steam. I would like each of you to choose one and put it on the right table. Use the objects already on the tables as clues to help you decide. I will carry the steaming saucepan for the Lab Cat who chooses it. We have to be careful – it is very, very hot."

When they had finished, the Prof cried, "Well done!"

"But Prof," asked Lucky. "What about jelly? When it's hot, jelly is runny like water. But when it has cooled down, it stays the same shape. So, is jelly a liquid or a solid?"

"It all depends on the temperature," said the Prof.

"Tempurr…ature?" asked Lucky – and started purring loudly again.

"That's enough of that," warned the Prof with a frown. "Pay attention and watch this!"

She went to the fridge and took out some ice cubes. She placed them in a saucepan and turned on the heat.

"Ice is a solid, right? Now look closely."

When we try something out, it is called an experiment. What do you think will happen next?

As they watched, the ice cubes melted.

"They've turned into water!" exclaimed Lucky. "They are liquid now."

"Ugh!" shivered Precious. "I hate water. When it rains, it makes my fur all wet."

A little while later the water started boiling.

"And now it is steam — a gas," declared Lucky.

"So, what do we learn from our little experiment?" asked the Prof.

"Something can be a solid, liquid or gas, depending on how hot or cold it is," said Swot.

"Yes. You can change a solid into a liquid by heating it, then change the liquid back to a solid by cooling it – the same with a liquid and a gas. Any other examples, Lab Cats?"

"Now find out what happens when you put things into water," said the Prof.

The cats soaked bread, paper and plastic in water. The bread became soft and soggy, and so did the paper.

But the plastic did not.

"Plastic does not soak up the water," explained the Prof. "So we call it *waterproof*."

Yuk!

A plastic coat keeps out the rain.

A tip for when you are washing dishes: soak them first to make the dried food stains go soft.

That's why drinks come in plastic bottles.

"Now each of you have a go at this experiment," said the Prof. "See what you notice."

They each filled a cup with warm water from the tap. Lucky poured sugar into her cup, Fluff chose sand, Swot dropped in some keys, Precious added sawdust, Basher stirred in salt, and Ginger put in a piece of chalk.

They stirred and stirred. Then Lucky and Basher noticed something surprising.

Keys

sugar

sand

sawdust

salt

chalk

What will happen to the things mixed with water in the cups?

The salt and sugar had disappeared!

"Salt and sugar dissolve in water – they become liquid," said the Prof. "You can't see them now, but they are still there. Have a taste."

They did so. Basher pulled a face. Lucky smacked her lips.

"If you heat the water, it will disappear – it will evaporate like puddles drying out on a hot day. The salt and sugar will then be left behind as white powders."

"I'll show you another disappearing trick," said the Prof. "I will do it for you because I don't want you playing with matches." She lit a candle.

As they watched, the burning candle became smaller and smaller. The wax was disappearing.

"The wax is changing into something else: invisible gases," explained the Prof. "This is not like the other changes we have seen. Once this has happened, it cannot be changed back."

"I'm hungry," growled Basher. "You've made us work so hard, we've been too busy to eat."

"Well, let's see what we can do about that," said the Prof. She got them to mix some flour, sugar, butter, eggs and water together to make a gooey mixture. They poured it into a baking tin and put it in the oven. While they were waiting for it to cook, the Prof broke some eggs into a frying pan and put them on the heat.

32

Science is everywhere – even in the kitchen.

In no time, the runny eggs became firm. The clear part had turned white.

"Another change that cannot be changed back," declared the Prof.

As for the dollop of gooey-looking mixture, when it was time to take it out of the oven, the Lab Cats were amazed to find it, too, had changed – into little cakes! They smelled delicious.

Basher wasn't the only hungry Lab Cat. They all joined in the midnight feast.

"Not only are you good scientists, but you are also good cooks," said the Prof. And when they had finished their meal, she added, in a no-nonsense tone of voice, "And now you will show me how good you are at washing up!"

See you next time for some more Science from the Prof and the Lab Cats!

Yummy!

Purr...fect!

HIC!

HIC!

What the words mean

Boiling: A liquid boils when it is heated and turns into bubbles of gas (for example, when water becomes steam).

Chemical change: When one kind of material changes into another and cannot be changed back, (for example, a burning candle turns to gas.

Dissolving: When a solid becomes a liquid when placed in another liquid (for example, salt in water).

Evaporating: When a liquid slowly changes into a gas (for example, a rain puddle drying out in the sun turns to vapour).

Experiment: Something we do to test a scientific idea (for example, seeing what happens when we heat ice cubes).

Freezing: When a liquid is cooled and becomes a solid (for example, water turning into ice cubes in the freezer).

Gases: Materials that can change their shape and size to fit any space (for example, air or steam).

Liquids: Materials that stay the same size but can change their shape to fit whatever they are placed in (for example, water in a bottle).

Materials: The stuff that things are made of (for example, wool, iron and wood).

Science: A knowledge of the world gained by looking carefully at things and trying out experiments.

Solids: Materials that stay the same shape and size (for example, a stone).

Temperature: How hot or cold something is.

Waterproof: If a material does not soak up water, it is waterproof.